Wiltshi[illegible] Radical History

Hanged at the scene of their crime

Angela Tuckett

West Country Rebels

Dame Florence Hancock

From Wiltshire to Westminster

Published by White Horse (Wiltshire) Trades Union Council.
Based on a series of talks given at a local history day school at The Cause, Chippenham on Saturday 29th March 2014.

Produced by Watermarx

Published in 2018
by
White Horse (Wiltshire) Trades Council

Produced by
WaterMarx
www.watermarx.co.uk

ISBN 978-0-9957917-0-1

Printed by Sarum Colourview
Unit 8, Woodford Centre
Lysander Way, Old Sarum, Salisbury SP4 6BU
01722 343600
www.sarumcolourview.co.uk

Disclaimer

Views expressed in this publication are those of the contributors and not necessarily those of WaterMarx or White Horse (Wiltshire) Trades Council

Contents

Cover picture: Combe Gibbet by Bob Naylor/WaterMarx©

Introduction

by Andy Newman
Chair, White Horse (Wiltshire) Trades Union Council

This book arose from the second history day organised by the White Horse Trades Union Council. We are a group of trade unionists in West Wiltshire, who get together to work on community and trades union projects. Our aim in organising these history day schools is to draw attention to the fact that major historical events have happened locally in Wiltshire.

The reason why I think these events are so important is that history is often presented - not only at school but also on the television and in popular culture - as things that important people do somewhere else. It all happens in London - or nowadays it all happens in Washington. But, actually, the most important struggles that have shaped our life and the world we live in were done by ordinary people in places just like this.

I would like to give credit to our trade union colleague, Dave Chappel, a postman from Bridgewater, who first suggested these history days to us, and who spoke at the first event we organised in Bradford on Avon in 2011. Actually, these history events have been easier to organise than I thought they would be. We quickly found that there are a number of people, not only professional academics but also local history buffs, and people in the trades union movement, who are really talented and knowledgeable about the history of their local towns.

We had the distinction of hosting Jeremy Corbyn speaking about his early upbringing in Chippenham, at a time before he had become a household name. Of course, Jeremy has always had a very strong reputation as a fighter for social justice among trade union activists, and his talk was particularly moving as he spoke with great affection about his friends and comrades, Tony Benn and Bob Crow, who had died only a short time before his talk.

I hope you enjoy this short book, as much as I have done.

Some of the audience at The Cause, Chippenham

Hanged at the scene of their crime

The gallows, the gibbet and the rural poor in Hanoverian Wiltshire

by Steve Poole
Professor of History and Heritage,
University of the West of England.

At the Wiltshire summer assize in 1813, two young labourers, George Ruddock (20) and George Carpenter (21) were capitally convicted for robbing and murdering a farmer and his servant in a house at Roddenbury Hill, near Warminster, and sentenced to death by hanging. This was not unusual in itself; an exemplary execution or two formed the closing drama to plenty of Wiltshire's twice yearly assize hearings in the eighteenth and nineteenth centuries.

But Ruddock and Carpenter's hanging was extraordinary because William Fowle, the High Sherriff, wanted them hanged as close as possible to the scene of their crime. Lying just over the county border, Roddenbury was beyond his jurisdiction so he settled instead for a nearby Wiltshire site with an appropriate view, Arn Hill, a 700 ft escarpment rising immediately behind Warminster.

From a logistical point of view, this was quite an enterprise. Fowle, Ruddock and Carpenter set out at 4.15 in the morning for the 21 mile journey from Fisherton gaol. They travelled in a hired mourning coach with a close escort of javelin men, cavalry and constables, the Under Sheriff and a clergyman. The Sheriff was anxious that everyone should get a good look at the faces of the condemned men as they passed. 'The coach drove slowly through the villages on the road to Warminster', it was reported, 'so that the inhabitants might have a view of the prisoners'. On arrival, Ruddock and Carpenter were taken out, marched to the marketplace and made to sit in a chapel to pray, then at 11am a more impressive procession of more than 300 people was formed up to escort them through town to the top of Arn Hill.

This required an expanded company of yeomanry, 100 bailiffs and constables, and the county javelin men as well as the Sheriff, the gaoler, the prison ordinary, a party of county magistrates, and the executioner. The condemned men marched beside their own coffins.

With what the Salisbury Journal called 'peculiar solemnity', this impressive procession took an hour and a half to make its way to the hilltop where a crowd of about 40,000 people were waiting, 'all of whom seemed properly impressed with the solemnity of the occasion'. The steep fall of the land allowed everyone 'to see it without pressure' and it allowed Ruddock and Carpenter to look beyond the crowd to Warminster churchyard where their victim was buried, and beyond that towards Roddenbury Hill, 'nearly in view of the house where the murderous deed was perpetrated'. There was no drop and trapdoor system to quicken their demise, just two posts and a crossbeam on the brow of the hill. Made to stand on the back of the cart with the ropes around their necks beneath the makeshift gallows, they were subjected to a further half hour of prayers, and then Carpenter was given a hanky and invited to drop it when they were both ready to die. A further 20 minutes elapsed: 'The poor wretch clung so close to life that he delayed dropping it for nearly half an hour, begging earnestly for a few minutes longer'.

Crime scene executions made no use of the relatively humane drop system, commonly in use at most nineteenth century public hangings. Instead the condemned were allowed to fall from the back of a moving cart, resulting in slow asphyxiation.

At length he let the hanky drop but even then 'endeavoured to prevent his fall, whereby he suffered greatly in dying'. People executed for murder at that time were forbidden Christian burial, so their bodies would either be left to rot on site in an iron gibbet cage, or handed over to the surgeons for anatomisation. Ruddock and Carpenter's bodies were accordingly gifted to Salisbury Infirmary.

If these procedures seem barbaric, it should be admitted that hanging people from the back of a cart at the scene of their crime was an odd thing to do in 19th century England. As the historian Pieter Spierenburg has put it, even by the dawn of the 'pre-industrial era... a regular location prevailed', a place of 'uni-locality' marking 'the routinizing of public punishment' throughout Europe and certainly in provincial England. By 1813, most 'regular locations' were established as close to the county gaol as possible; often on top of the gatehouse roof, with a relatively fast trapdoor mechanism for despatching the prisoner.

This meant doing away with the traditional practice of carting condemned men and women by procession to a place on the outskirts of town, where large crowds could

Like Ruddock and Carpenter in 1813, a condemned 18th century felon waits beneath the gallows for the execution cart to be pulled away. His death will not be quick. From an eighteenth century broadside (author's collection).

completely surround the gallows and come almost within touching distance of it.

At a time of increasing concerns about disorderly and disrespectful crowd behaviour at public hangings, centralisation sacrificed display and interaction with the crowd to the pressing demands of increased efficiency, speed, economy, and proper regulation.[1]

In London, this process was completed as early as 1783 when processions from Newgate to Tyburn were abandoned and executions performed outside the gaol instead.

Wiltshire's traditional 'Tyburn' had been sited at a road junction just beyond the Fisherton turnpike on the outskirts of Salisbury, but in 1796, this too was scrapped in favour of the yard of Fisherton gaol, at the southern end of Fisherton Street.

Because it was quicker, the drop has sometimes been linked to enlightenment ideas about rational moral 'improvement' and civilised behaviour. But this is simplistic. To call a revised plan of public execution 'more civilised' just because it happens more quickly, anonymously, 'efficiently' and at a greater distance from its audience, is not a definition of civilised behaviour all of us would share and it might be more accurate to say it was done to give a greater degree of control to the authorities and appease the squeamish.

In Wiltshire, some executions at the old gallows had certainly been haphazard and undignified, as the miserable death of a poor woman named Eleanor Hudd in 1783 demonstrates clearly enough. Condemned for infanticide but swearing to the last that her baby had been still-born, Hudd was 'so weak and insensible before she was taken from the prison as to be incapable of receiving any spiritual assistance, no clergyman therefore attended her at the place of execution, nor were her arms pinioned. On the cart drawing away then, she suddenly caught hold of the rope and supported herself for some time till her hands could be forced from their hold'.[2]

Inconveniences like these would not be experienced at the new drop. But, whatever the reason for centralising the process in 1796, one might surely have expected it to bring an end to the antiquated practice of carting condemned felons across miles of open country to be roughly strangled at the scene of their crime. Carpenter and Ruddock's hanging at Warminster in 1813 is one of many cases across the country that tell us it didn't. In fact, the last crime scene hanging in England, following a complicated 42 mile procession across country from Ilchester, took place at Kenn, Somerset, as late as 1830.

Let's spell it out: Crime scene hangings don't sit easily with progressive ideas about the forward march of civilised values. Most were in rural locations on makeshift apparatus with inexperienced local hangmen and no drop system. Most required lengthy and expensive processions. And if one purpose in shifting executions to the county gaol was to make them as quick, regular and anonymous as possible, crime scene executions did the opposite, for they emphasised personal association with the local landscapes on which they took place.

England witnessed a little over 200 crime scene hangings between 1720 and 1830. The great majority of victims were men and many were also gibbeted on the spot. It's a tiny proportion of the total number hanged (there were 7000 executions in England and Wales between 1770 and 1830 alone), but it's the consistency of them, in a supposed age of humanitarian reform that seems anomalous.

The geographical distribution of these cumbersome rituals was uneven; most took place in the South East where the Surrey assize was responsible for the greatest number of convictions, but there were high numbers in parts of the South West as well. Cornwall saw none, Devon just two but Somerset and Gloucestershire ordered nineteen between them. The highest number in any single Western County were organised by the Sheriffs of Wiltshire. This county hanged eleven men in this way, at eight separate sites.

Like many of those in other counties, the Wiltshire hangings have several features in common. Virtually all of them were ordered in peripheral rural districts, close to the borders and at some distance from 'the usual place'; amongst communities, in other words, who rarely or never directly witnessed capital punishment. All of the Wiltshire sample were carried out upon poor men convicted of robbing (and in all but two cases, murdering) their social superiors. The decision to order them was invariably a local one since site selection for any public hanging rested with the High Sheriff, unless specifically chosen by the judge. Clearly stated explanations were rarely given – in some cases close to Wiltshire, it seems to have been the relationship between economic and social crime that tipped the balance. Ely Hatton, put to death at Mitcheldeane, Gloucestershire, in 1732 for instance, was condemned for a murder he swore to the last he had not committed, although he freely admitted being a frequenter of brothels, a Sabbath breaker and a poacher of the squire's deer.

Samuel Yendall, hanged outside the gates of Pyrland Hall, Somerset in 1788, was also a poacher, though it was specifically violent assault and robbery that brought him to the gallows. Yendall farmed land rented from the magistrate and squire of Pyrland Hall, Sir William Yea. He and some of his friends, who had been embroiled in a row with Yea over gaming rights for some months, broke into his house one night, threatened him with a pistol, tied him up and gave him a severe beating. Clearly this was not the approved way of approaching a respected member of the county's magistracy. 'Men, women and children have all been conspirators', advised the Bath Chronicle, 'The whole country is in an uproar... Deer have been killed early in the morning if the Baronet was at home, or shot openly in the middle of the day if absent'.[3] Yendall was convicted and hanged at the scene of his crime, and Yea attended in person, 'causing the hangman to turn him round several times, being extended twenty feet high' to ensure everyone got a good look at his face.

Not far from the place where Ruddock and Carpenter were put to death in 1813, another two young labourers, Matthew Gardener and John Wheeler, had been hanged for robbery in 1783. Not only had they chosen a farmer returning with bulging pocket books from Warminster market, but they were also believed to be members of a criminal gang responsible for a number of break-ins around Warminster. Worse yet, these robberies had not been stopped by Gardener and Wheeler's arrest. So, in the same year that London's Tyburn procession was exchanged for the Newgate drop, Gardener and Wheeler were carted from Salisbury to a patch of ground beside what is now the Warminster by-pass at Blacketts copse on Sutton common, with the clear intention of striking terror into their associates in the surrounding villages. 'It is to be hoped', declared the local paper, 'that this shocking spectacle, so unusual in this neighbourhood, will be a warning to the rest of the gang, who have continued to infest and terrify the inhabitants of Warminster ever since the arrest of their confederates.'

Where crime scene executions occasionally followed serious outbreaks of riot and disorder, it was more often on the instructions of the assize judge than the county sheriff. Local authority figures generally erred on the side of caution lest a hanging ordered within a disaffected community only cause further disorder. Twenty five executions were effected in various parts of London after the Gordon Riots of 1780, and one at Bath too, but the execution of seven striking coalheavers at Wapping in 1768 had required the deployment of 600 soldiers and two divisions of constables to keep a hostile crowd at bay. When government required two silk weavers to be hanged at Bethnal Green the following year, again after industrial unrest, the city Sheriffs objected. They were over-ruled and the executions took place but there was fierce retaliatory rioting. Arguments of this kind followed the Birmingham Church and King riots of 1791, the Luddite outbreaks in Yorkshire in 1813, and the Captain Swing rebellion in Southern England in 1830. On each of these occasions, cold feet prevailed and crime scene hangings were not pursued. Unsurprisingly, in any debate about whether or not to stage an exemplary execution of this kind, the deciding factor was the assumption of an acquiescent crowd.

'Nothing seems to me a more likely means of restoring confidence than the delinquents being speedily tried and punished, if convicted, at the place where the offence arose', argued the Town Clerk of Bath after Gordon rioting in the town had caused a mass exodus of horrified wealthy visitors in 1780. The Attorney General agreed. 'It may be proper for the sake of example', he wrote, 'to bring convicts to Bath for execution on this occasion'. The assize judge obliged and a young Royal Crescent footman named John Butler, singled out as a scapegoat by the local administration, became the only person ever to be hanged at Bath this side of the Monmouth Rebellion.[4]

Contemporary accounts of crime scene hangings frequently stress the exemplary behaviour of all actors in the drama, from the cowed remorse of the penitent felon, to the sympathetic disposition of unprecedentedly large crowds gathered in witness, and the upright, solicitous and commanding demeanour of the Sheriff and his retinue. Butler's crowd, it was said, wept openly in the streets as his family joined him in the cart for his journey to the gallows. Some fourteen thousand people reportedly watched William Amor, being executed and gibbeted on Pewsey Down in 1773 for the murder there of a tailor. 'In the course of his journey to the place of execution, he confessed himself to be very penitent... His wife met him on Pewsey Down by his own desire, and their separation was, on her part, uncommonly affecting'.

Confronted once again with the scene of their crime, and by people from their own communities, public confession and an acceptance of the just workings of the law could be hoped for. Strenuous efforts might be made to entice expressions of contrition. Some obliged by admitting their guilt as the procession arrived; others were less compliant. John Curtis was ordered for execution and gibbeting on Harnham Hill just South of Salisbury in 1768. His supposed crime was the murder and robbery of a Jewish pedlar called Wolf Myers, but the evidence was circumstantial and Curtis denied the charge throughout. Brought within sight of the 26 foot high gibbet on which he was soon to be strung up, Curtis was first ordered to be 'carried around the pit into which he threw the body and asked if he remembered the place', but the desired confession was not forthcoming.

Wiltshire's last crime scene execution was ordered for Robert Watkins, convicted of shooting and robbing a coal merchant in the tiny hamlet of Stoke Purton near Swindon in 1819. He was a poor labourer, with three children to feed and whose wife had recently died. It seems he ambushed his wealthy victim on an impulse as he rode home to Wootten Bassett with a full wallet. Impertinent and careless in court, Watkins was ordered for execution at the crime scene by the assize judge. 'The number of persons in the road and neighbouring fields was immense', it was reported, the crowd expressing, 'a fearful and breathless anxiety, a solemn stillness, and a deep expression of melancholy thought... Near to the fatal spot, the cart passed his wretched mother. He looked steadfastly at her for some moments and with a gentle inclination of head and great expression of feature, seemed to take an eternal farewell of her'.

Even in 1830 after the hanging of three men in a Somerset village for setting fire to a farmer's hay ricks, the Methodist minister John Leifchild was impressed by the dramatic and familial tragedy that unfolded before him: 'What occasion had these men for deep sorrow and regret when brought for the last time to witness scenes familiar to them from their infancy', he wrote,' how often may they have paced this very spot in the innocence of childhood!'[5]

These complex, lengthy and stage-managed events have little in common with either the disorderly culture of London's Tyburn or any of the more speedily conducted and anonymous rituals staged at county gaols. So-called 'carnivalesque' crowd responses to execution in London have sometimes been interpreted as a form of popular protest – of refusal to be humbled by the bloody code, or made penitent by the bullying force of the Law. But if so, it was a response learned over time through familiarity with the Law's procedures and developed slowly into a culture of everyday resistance. No such repertoires of protest had been learned in the countryside, in places that had never witnessed a hanging before.

The irregularity of crime scene hangings was partly an effect of their expense. On poor rural roads, processions across country might take many hours to accomplish and the expense of guarding the cart and equipping the gallows was often considerable. By contrast, executions were not particularly expensive if carried out with minimal fuss at the 'usual place', close to the county gaol. The average cost of dieting, guarding and hanging a felon conventionally in mid eighteenth century Gloucestershire was five guineas for example and in Wiltshire it was three.

But some much higher expenses were recorded in the execution and gibbeting of a sailor named William Jacques at Stanton St Quintin near Chippenham in 1764. This hanging cost the Sheriff of Wiltshire a hefty £28.00, as set out in his annual cravings (his expenses claim) to the Exchequer. The account first itemises horse hire and an exploratory journey with sundry expenses for visiting the district in advance, 'forty miles distant from Sarum', to select a suitable spot. Then, for the hanging itself there was cart hire, the gaoler's travel expenses, and security from interference by the prisoner's friends and family to consider. Sums were required 'for the under sheriff's journey and all his Bailiffs and for horse hire and expenses to guard and attend

Crime scene hangings were often located on adjacent hill tops which offered prominent vantage points for the gibbet and unencumbered views for large audiences

the execution for fear the sailors should come from Bristol and rescue him, he being a sailor from Bristol, not being far from Stanton', and then finally for ordering, transporting and fixing the gibbet cage.

The exceptional nature of events like these attracted unusually large crowds, but sheriffs were usually able to manage and accommodate them in a remarkably orderly manner. Given open landscapes that presented none of the congestion difficulties intrinsic to London executions, vantage points could be carefully chosen for their spatial and topographical significance, and temporary gallows of great height constructed to ensure uninterrupted views from a distance.

High vantage points drew attention from miles around even in remote locations, and offered county authorities unparalleled opportunities to parade in full regalia before enormous audiences for whom pageantry of any kind was a novelty. And time was not an issue. For people and Sheriff, deliberately unhurried ceremonies only confirmed the paternal nature of decentralised authority. The longer the ceremony took to accomplish, the more distressing the scene as families and communities bade their final farewells, the more deeply it became embedded in local memory. The intention of any crime scene execution, of course, was to leave an indelible psychic mark upon place and community and if folklore and reliquary are anything to go by, this was invariably achieved. Certainly the material culture of execution can be recorded from numerous slivers of wood taken as souvenirs from gallows and in surviving community memory concerning hanging sites. Although the bodies of Carpenter and Ruddock were not gibbeted but delivered to the surgeons at Salisbury Infirmary, a trophy cut from Carpenter survives to this day in the memorabilia collection of a London funeral company.

This was the young labourer's right arm, severed from his body after execution at the request of a Warminster surgeon and preserved in a labelled box as a memento of a remarkable event.

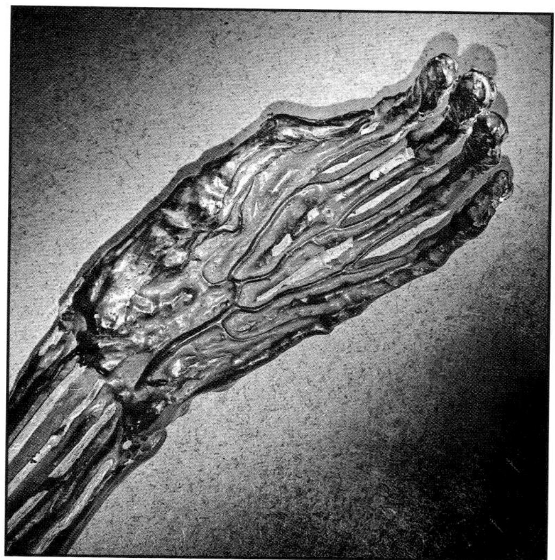

The mummified hand of George Carpenter, cut from his body after execution and preserved as a grisly souvenir by a local surgeon (Thomas Cribb and sons, London).

Robert Watkins's hanging at Purton Stoke in 1819 is commemorated by the survival of the name 'Watkins Corner' at a bend in the road beside the execution site, the inscribed prayer book from which the condemned man read as he prepared himself for death, and a village re-enactment in 2007, complete with souvenir mugs.

Crime scene hangings finally came to an end in 1830, not because they were deemed uncivilised but because central government steadily became more reluctant to reimburse sheriffs beyond a standard fee. By the close of the Napoleonic Wars, the uniformity of execution practices in most counties allowed the Crown to create a fixed allowance to sheriffs of £2.00 per felon, a sum somewhat out of touch with inflation, even for quick and simple executions at the 'usual place'. Despite the serious post-war recession, this fee remained standard between 1815 and 1830. Ministers took the view that higher cravings had been tolerated in the previous century because 'government was not yet thought stable and the times were perilous'. In the more secure nineteenth century, they argued, execution cravings in excess of £2.00 were permissible only in anticipation of serious disorder and attempted rescue – but these phenomena should never be expected. The signal was clear enough – exemplary crime scene executions carried out at extra expense but in otherwise orderly rural communities, would no longer be paid for. Sheriffs who protested were reminded that the position they held conferred the highest honour upon them and that 'in a free country, the highest privileges have their correlative burdens'.

In Hanoverian England, however, whatever the expense and despite a parallel urge to modernise, county sheriffs and assize judges alike understood that the much maligned 'great moral lesson' of the scaffold was still capable of working its magic in places where familiarity, locality and community still retained the power to serve the interests of the judicial State.

Further Reading

This short essay draws upon two longer publications by the same author:
'A lasting and salutary warning: Incendiarism, Rural Order and England's Last Scene of Crime Execution', *Rural History (2008)* **19**(2) pp163-177 and 'For the Benefit of Example: Crime Scene Executions in England, 1720-1830', in King, P and Ward, R (eds), *A Global History of Execution and the Criminal Corpse* (London: Palgrave) 2015, pp71-101.

Footnotes

1. Pieter Spierenburg, *The Spectacle of Suffering. Executions and the evolution of repression: from a pre-industrial metropolis to the European experience* (Cambridge: Cambridge University Press) 1984, p45.

2. *Bath Chronicle* 13 August 1783

3. *Bath Chronicle* 12 August 1779; 6 March 1788. Another eleven of the suspected poaching gang were taken up under the game laws following the assault on Yea.

4. The National Archive, State Papers (TNASP) 37/21/155; *Jefferys to Lord Hillsborough*, 18 June 1780; TNASP 37/21/257, *Mr Attorney General's Report on the Mode of Trying the Rioters at Bath*, 15 July 1780; *Bath Journal* 31 August 1780. On the London executions, see Rogers, Nicholas (2011) *Calibrating Justice in the Gordon Riots of 1780*, unpublished paper.

5. Rev J Leifchild DD (1967) *Remarkable Facts Illustrative and Confirmatory of Different Portions of Holy Scripture* (London) p222. For this event see Poole, Steve (2008) A lasting and salutary warning: Incendiarism, rural order and England's last scene of crime execution, *Rural History* **19** (2) pp163-177.

Angela Remembered

The Life and Times of Angela Gradwell Tuckett

by Rosie MacGregor

Angela was a commanding figure, tall and angular with a strong face. She was a complex character with a history of militancy and radical politics whose disparate experiences encompassed playing hockey for England, qualifying as the first female solicitor in Bristol, writing for various left-wing publications, as well as writing books, plays, songs and poems, singing and playing concertina. All pursued with the same unswerving passion she had felt when joining the Communist Party as a young woman.

Early years

Angela Mary Tuckett was born in 1906 into an affluent household in Clifton, Bristol. Her father Richard Clapson Tuckett was a local solicitor and her mother was Edna Mary Stacy. Angela had two older siblings, a sister Joan and a brother Coldstream. Angela's mother died when she was born but she was nurtured in a large and loving family, many of whom were eminent Bristolian Quakers including her grandfather Coldstream Tuckett, a tea merchant who ran a grocery business and lived in Stokes Croft in what is still known as Tuckett's Buildings.

Angela on the left with her father, brother and sister (courtesy Working Class Movement Library)

She grew up in a progressive and creative home where she was encouraged to think for herself and take an interest in art and politics. Her mother's sister, Enid, who died before Angela was born, was a well-known socialist and a campaigner for women's rights, a founding member of the Independent Labour Party and a member of the Gasworkers' Union who took part in the Bristol Cotton Workers' Strike of 1890.

Angela's grandfather on her mother's side was Henry Stacy who taught art at Bristol University and had a studio in Cotham. He was a leading member of a group of artists known as The Bristol Savages and knew many of the artists and intellectuals of the day who were regular visitors to his studio including George Bernard Shaw and Eleanor Marx. A trade union banner painted by Henry for the Gasworkers' Union is still in existence today. Angela's earliest

Clifton High School Hockey 1st XI, Angela on the right of centre row (courtesy Working Class Movement Library)

childhood memory was of sitting on Emmeline Pankhurst's knee in her grandfather's studio!

Angela attended the progressive Clifton High School, a private girl's school a short walk from her home. She excelled both academically and at sport, especially hockey and was a member of the school's 1st XI. Expected to go to Oxford, she had other ideas and left school aged 16 in the autumn of 1922 and was articled to her father's Bristol based legal practice.

The plight of the unemployed in Bristol and the 1931 Welsh Hunger Marches were to have a profound effect on Angela and she joined the Communist Party of Great Britain, taking food and copies of the Daily Worker to the marchers each day. She soon became active organising meetings, acting as a driver, and becoming 'legal observer' at demonstrations, including facing baton charges by the police at two violent demonstrations in Old Market, Bristol in 1932. Angela states that an 'immense crowd' gathered and 'were suddenly set upon by posses of police who had been hiding in shop doors and side alleys whilst mounted police charged up from Old Market Street and laid into them. Angela's legal expertise proved useful in defending the leaders of the National Unemployed Workers Movement who had been arrested for incitement. She was 'frequently in demand in South Wales where police violence was getting out of hand and the courts were imposing savage sentences on demonstrators'.

Old Market riot in Bristol in 1932

Marriage and travel

She met her first husband John Gustave Pilley in 1929, seven years her senior, a university lecturer and Marxist theorist. Their physical relationship soon after they met resulted in what she later described as 'undergoing a nightmare backstreet abortion'. Pilley widened her knowledge of life and politics but it was ultimately a destructive relationship. He had visited Russia in the summer of 1931 and returned 'more vocal than ever on Marxist theory' but to Angela's exasperation he refused to join the Communist Party or any other left-wing organisation.

John had been one of the most promising students of his generation at Oxford and through him she met other gifted young Oxford graduates like Hugh Gaitskell and John Strachey and was initially impressed not just by his intelligence but his wide circle of influential friends. Angela, who was only twenty-three when they met, was perhaps a little infatuated with her older and more experienced lover and the glamorous new world of politics and academia to which she was being introduced.

They married in 1933 and moved into a flat in Worcester Terrace but she was already having doubts as their relationship deteriorated. He did not regard her as his intellectual equal and despised her lack of knowledge of Marxist theory. Numerous visits to London followed where John could have some 'intelligent conversation' with 'real intellectuals' like 'Sage' Bernal and Naomi Mitchison where those present would be 'hanging on every word about the meaning of revolutionary theory'. Angela found these 'dreary gatherings' incredibly boring. The prolonged theoretical conversations of these intellectuals with no proposals for action both puzzled and worried Angela as they bore no relationship to the everyday reality of the hardships people were experiencing.

It was at one of these gatherings that she first met the renowned politician, barrister and Soviet sympathiser DN Pritt who like Angela did not find these meetings particularly enlightening. She worked with him on a number of cases and recalled one instance when they had been defending unemployed miners in Monmouthshire charged with 'riot and assault' after police with batons had viciously broken up a large demonstration. The miners were cleared of assault but convicted of riot and sent to gaol.

Perhaps to distract her, John Pilley entered her name in a newspaper competition to receive flying lessons, and to her surprise she won. It was a new challenge that she greatly enjoyed, receiving lessons at the Bristol Airfield just off the Wells Road and was allowed to fly solo after less than 5 hours flying time and after less than 16 flying hours she took her test and passed.

Throughout the 1920s and 30s Angela travelled widely across Europe and to USA, most notably during the Spanish Civil War as an activist and propagandist in support of the Spanish Republic. There were visits to the South of France, Corsica, Spain, Greece and Cyprus. In those days of fast emerging fascism Angela was only too aware of the growing economic, political, racial and national tensions.

Angela was part of the England Ladies Hockey Team who played in

Germany in 1935 in a stadium designed and being made ready for the Olympics the following year. Angela was horrified that the Nazis viewed this event as a mechanism to gain publicity for their regime. General von Blomberg was deputising for Hitler when the English team passed through a cordon of Hitler youth all giving the Nazi salute as the team entered the stadium.

Angela alone, despite having been told she must, did not return their salute and was subsequently evasive with the German press. The next day Angela was told that complaints had been received at the highest level and she was reprimanded by a hostile team manager. Despite having been one of the most successful players in the team, playing International Hockey from 1931 until 1935, she was never selected to play for England again.

In the spring of 1936 Angela joined her husband on a lecture tour of the Greek Islands and was amazed to see many political slogans with hammer and sickle symbols painted on the high walls in the poorer working class areas of Athens. They returned in the spring of 1937 when at considerable risk she was persuaded to take 'red aid' to Greece in the form of dollars stashed inside her concertina. The shop in Piraeus Harbour where the money was to have been delivered had shut. Uncertain what to do Angela went to where on a previous visit she had seen Communist slogans but these had now been whitewashed out.

She sat dejectedly on the kerb in the deserted street. A small group of children began to show an interest in her but spoke no English. She pointed at the patch on the wall where the slogan had been then traced a hammer and sickle with her finger in the dust and made the sign of a clenched fist. One of the older children took her hand and led her to a nearby house where a woman took her in her arms and arranged to deliver the money.

On return to England John received the offer of a year's sabbatical at New York University. Although there were numerous difficulties in the marriage and she knew he had been unfaithful, she felt that a change of environment might result in a fresh start and agreed to go with him. His extramarital relationships had been casual affairs, or so she thought, but as Angela said farewell to family and friends, he was in Paris with the woman who was to become his second wife.

On 27 August 1937 John and Angela took the train to Liverpool to catch the boat to New York. Even as the train left Bristol they were no longer speaking to each other and once they had embarked she wished she had remained in England.

Bored and lonely in America she was desperate for something to occupy the hours. She made contact with the Society for Cultural Relations with the Soviet Union but found it was 'rather more cultural than socialist'. She thought the North American Committee for Spanish Relief was more plausible but discovered that it functioned merely to hold fund raising cocktail parties!

She continued to look for something to fill the void and found herself arranging a sale of authors' manuscripts for the League of American Writers to raise aid for the Spanish struggles. She rapidly made friends with a number of left-wing writers and was impressed by the radical theatre productions she saw in New York.

The political situation in Europe was becoming more volatile and war seemed inevitable. Pilley had secured a second year's sabbatical to go to Wellesley College in Boston, Massachusetts. Many of the English then living in America were seeking to evade war by remaining in USA but this did not suit Angela. Recognising that her marriage was over she returned to Britain in July 1939. They divorced two years later.

Bristol Unity Players

She never severed her links with Bristol and both Angela and her sister Joan were members of the League of Progressive Writers and stalwarts of Bristol's Unity Players Club. Joan was producer from 1935 until 1947 co-writing numerous plays with Angela including *The Bulls see Red* about the Spanish Civil War.

Despite frequent air raids and casualties within the players, the club continued to put on performances throughout the Second World War. The Unity Players performed in theatres and prominent public places including the Colston Hall and open-air stages on the Downs and in Queen Square, attended by thousands and always in protest or in celebration of some significant event in the socialist calendar.

The London Years

Angela's first job on return to England was, out of necessity, as a finance clerk in a large London office where she quickly discovered how hierarchical such places were and that a culture of bullying existed openly in the workplace.

Always a feisty woman she stood up to the bullying and as she was already a trade union member she encouraged others to join. This did not please the management and it wasn't long before she received a letter saying her services were no longer required.

Bombs began to fall on London when war began but Angela, fearless as ever, was determined to remain in the city.

She was appointed Head of the Legal Department of the National Council for Civil Liberties (now Liberty) in 1940. It was a natural progression for someone with a legal training, sharp mind, good judgement, astute understanding of politics and belief in equality. Angela immersed herself in her new role as refugees were treated as enemy aliens, unfair detention without any explanation or trial was commonplace, and even when there was a hearing, it was in secret with no right to a legal advisor, and questions were being raised about the freedom of the press. People were being victimised simply for expressing an adverse opinion or comment.

She joined The Daily Worker as its solicitor and legal advisor in 1942 working also as a reporter and subsequently sub-editor and joined the National Union of Journalists.

She was at work on the morning of 6 August 1945 and so she was one of the first to hear that America had dropped the atomic bomb on Hiroshima. This made her even more determined and resolute in her belief in peace and disarmament.

Angela continued to work for The Daily Worker until 1948 when she moved to Labour Monthly where she remained for another 30 years working as a sub-editor.

The Move to Swindon

An entirely new chapter opened in her life when she met Ike Gradwell on an official visit to Czechoslovakia in 1961 and they married in 1962. It was a second marriage for both and those who knew them from that time variously described them as 'soul-mates', 'like-minded' and 'a devoted couple' not just to each other but equally committed to the various causes they supported. They were both strong personalities, each with a dogged determination to fight for principles they shared, but equally kind and understanding, which may explain why their relationship with each other was such a success. It was a marriage of equals. Angela described Ike Gradwell as 'the love of her life'.

Ike was a Swindon based joiner and craft teacher, who was an activist within the NUT, Swindon Communist Party and the Peace Movement. Like Angela, Ike was born in 1906, and though their family backgrounds were entirely different, they had many other things in common. They both had indefatigable energy combined with intelligence and a quick mind, a desire to work hard and influence others and shared beliefs in a better system in which peace and equality were paramount.

She said of an official visit to the Soviet Union with Ike in 1962 that one of the most impressive trips had been to the Volga Hydroelectric Station. After which they went for a swim in the river whilst 'Volga boatmen steered vast rafts of felled timber past them'. Angela commented that the river water was yellow and 'tasted of thick soup'!

Angela stood as a Communist in the Wiltshire Council elections in 1967. She failed to win but surprisingly succeeded

Campaigning with Ike on the streets of Swindon

in gaining 7.4% of the poll, which in a town then dominated by Labour and a county dominated by the Conservatives is no mean feat.

Many remember Angela busking on the streets of Swindon, attending rallies and demonstrations and selling *The Morning Star* no matter how good or bad the weather. She was a distinctive figure singing and playing her concertina to raise funds for the peace movement and in the mid-1980s for striking miners and their families - always wearing a miner's helmet with a 'borrowed' Tesco's shopping trolley filled with banners, placards and leaflets. She would wheel it down to the centre of town and stay there all day and play her concertina most of the time 'whether or not people wanted to hear from her'.

She was also a regular visitor to Greenham Common. Regularly performing at local folk clubs and festivals, singing and playing her concertina, she rarely missed The Singer's Club in Swindon on Friday evenings, founded in 1960 by fellow communists Ted and Ivy Poole. She was a member for more than 30 years until her death.

She wrote a number of major works of non-fiction including *The Scottish Carter* published in 1967, *The Blacksmiths History* published in 1974 and *The Scottish Trades Union Congress: The First 80 Years 1897-1977,* published in 1986.

The Blitz and the misery it caused horrified Angela but also inspired her to write poetry. *Verses Against Fascism and War* is a collection of poems about the years of fascist dictatorships of the 1930s and 40s ending with peace. The first written in 1934 and eventually published as a collection in December 1979. And she also published her own song books.

Angela had no alternative due to failing health but to move first to an elderly person's home in her final years and finally to hospital where she died in August 1994 at the age of 88. Once installed in the elderly person's home 'she would be out of the door, often first thing in the morning after breakfast, for a walk along the old canal or through the park. Despite infirmity she would walk miles and just keep going until she was too tired to continue, at which point she would flag down any car and ask bewildered strangers to give her a lift home. Either too polite to turn her down, or worried about her health, the request worked without fail! Her many friends even formed an 'escape committee' to ensure that she could continue to visit all the local folk clubs.

There is a commemorative bench close to the bandstand in Swindon's Town Gardens and a simple plaque that reads 'Angela Gradwell 1905 – 1994 who dedicated her life to international peace and solidarity. From Swindon Communists and Friends'.

Whatever views people may have about Marxist theory and communist ideology, the successes or the failures and disappointments that history has shown us in their implementation, especially during Stalin's regime, Angela must be admired for her unswerving devotion to the cause. Though having committed so much of her life to this cause it would have been difficult if not impossible to retract. She will be remembered as an inspirational character with boundless energy who had never waivered in her belief that a fairer and more equal society was achievable. A peaceful society in which wealth was more evenly distributed, where no one need go hungry and where art and music were not merely the prerogative of the wealthy but accessible to all to live a happy and fulfilled life. She had worked ceaselessly throughout a long and eventful life seeking to achieve this goal.

Postscript

It was inevitable after completing this short biography that people would bring forward new stories about her, including confirmation of some that had seemed too implausible. Several people told me that Angela, always the keen athlete, was more agile into her 80s than most people less than half her age. She exercised every day and was still able to do 'the splits' and 'turn cartwheels'. She was always slim, very nimble and held her body upright without the slightest evidence of a stoop. Even so it seemed improbable since I had never seen her give a display. Many of those who mentioned it said they had only heard it in passing from others so I didn't include any mention in my book. Since then many more have verified this,

Angela wearing a miner's helmet supporting their strike

having actually seen her give a demonstration, and I now have no doubt that it is true. Equally improbable to many was Angela's great sense of humour but I can imagine her wicked smile as she exhibited these gymnastic accomplishments.

A case finally solved! I mentioned her clandestine activities of liberating food from a government depot near Swindon when giving a talk about the book to a group in Chippenham. The liberated food was then taken to South Wales and distributed amongst striking miners and their families. After my talk a retired Chief Superintendent who had known Angela gave a vote of thanks and told an amusing anecdote. He had been a Detective Inspector with the Swindon Division of Wiltshire Police in the mid 1980s and had been sent with others to investigate the theft of food from that same government depot. They had never been able to solve the mystery and he was greatly amused that at last, too late to press charges, he had discovered the truth and solved the crime, thirty years after the event! He added that Angela and her associates were well known to the police. I'm not entirely sure what he meant by that statement, though I understand he had also worked with Special Branch!

I have been surprised by the number of people who have contacted me to say how much they enjoyed reading the book. Some said it brought memories flooding back. Others that it had given them more of an insight into someone they regarded as a sad and lonely eccentric, without realising what a full life she had led, and now felt a greater sympathy towards her memory. Earlier one of these had said 'You don't mean the strange old lady who used to wear a miner's hat whilst playing a concertina on a roundabout in Swindon' when I asked if they had known her! I am certain she was lonely towards the end of her life which may explain why she was constantly on the move and rarely at home. Preferring to be in the company of others or out walking. I don't believe this devalues the memory of her as a strong and resolute woman, merely that loneliness, especially following the death of a partner, is an affliction suffered by too many in old age.

Another who knew her well through folk music told me that Angela was always a little too willing to argue and discuss the deeper meaning and interpretation of traditional folk songs, often finding, however implausibly, a political aspect that only she could decipher. Yet we all put our own interpretation based on our own experience onto songs we have heard, books we have read and plays we have seen. Angela may have been correct since early folk songs, particularly broadside ballads, were often written in response to a social or political situation and the meanings deliberately concealed to prevent them being understood by those in power or authority. Another person remembered that it was impossible to win an argument with Angela "best not to try"!

I made many attempts during my research to contact England Hockey about Angela but received no response to my letters. However, following publication I was contacted by a representative of the new Hockey Museum. It transpires that Angela played for England in no less than 11 Hockey Internationals and was 'a fast and effective forward'. She even wrote for the Women's Hockey Magazine 'where she had a page and carte blanche to write as she wanted'! Various reports mention Angela and her ill-fated final game for her country when England beat Germany 6 - 3.

One of the Trustees of the Hockey Museum told me that 'in the following season she was still on outstanding form and played in the England v The Rest game in the November and in all the territorial games but did not appear in any of the selected England teams or reserves announced in Feb 1936. The Hockey Field magazine editorial notes that "...Mrs Pilley does not even appear in the reserves list this year – surely the biggest surprise of all. According to reports from the territorial matches, Mrs Pilley has been up to form and lost none of her speed and initiative." This does seem to support Angela's story that she upset the 'hierarchy' with her refusal to give the Nazi salute and in her answers to the press after the game. That said, I have been involved with sport all my life and have experienced many strange selection decisions, so it is possible to argue incompetence rather than conspiracy!'

Much to my delight I was contacted by the son of Angela's first husband John Pilley, one of two boys from his second marriage, who had read a review of the book. Angela had featured in family photos and films taken by his father, some even showing Angela turning somersaults. He sent me a photograph of a good looking couple, his father seated with his mother in a pavement cafe in Paris in 1937 when they visited the International Exhibition. Ironically this was the same trip when Angela was left alone at home packing ready to embark with John to The States. I wonder if this might have been the cause of the rows that Angela mentions in her diary notes. There is another photograph of his mother with Charles Evans, his father's old friend from Oxford on the same visit to Paris. Charles Evans later married Robin Page Arnot's daughter Barbara with whom Angela had once shared a flat and through this connection links with Angela were maintained. Another photo shows a happy Angela with John taken in 1929. John's son confirmed that his father had several affairs during the 1930s including with the writer Naomi Mitchison from 1931 – 33 who was at the time married with young children. John's son had assumed that his father's first marriage was an intellectual, rather avant-garde, left wing 'open marriage'. I doubt the young Angela saw it in quite the same context but looking at the photographs of a handsome John Pilley it is easy to understand why women fell so easily in love with him.

Further Reading: *Angela Remembered* by Rosie MacGregor.
Published by WaterMarx 2015.
ISBN 978-0-9570726-3-3

West Country Rebels

by Nigel Costley,
Regional Secretary South West TUC

One of the reasons that I was so compelled to produce a digest of West Country Rebels was that actually the more you dig into history the more emerges. I don't claim to do justice to the stories that are still out there that still need to be written. I think they are the most hidden part of our social history. The West Country is a beautiful part of the country, it's where you go on holiday to or if you're lucky to retire to. It is politically on the right of centre but if you scratch the surface it has been a region at the heart of many a rebellion and uprising and has spawned many a trouble maker. I thought it was important that we remember them.

Rebellion in Cornwall

What has become known as the Cornish Rebellion started over unfair taxes from London and it spread in 1497 from Cornwall led by Michael An Gof, a blacksmith from the Lizard, and Thomas Flamank from Bodmin. Although it's called the Cornish Rebellion it actually brought with it people from Devon and Somerset. There were lots of West Country folk who joined this march on the capital and when they arrived in London the King was concerned that this was a rebellion that was going to be successful.

Unfortunately it was brutally put down. But a year later, despite the tragic end to the first rebellion, another uprising starts in Cornwall led by Perkin Warbeck – an upstart with claims of royal heritage. It didn't get anywhere near the capital and it marched from Land's End up as far as Taunton before the King's troops put it down.

Another rebellion, now called the Prayer Book Rebellion started over the rights of worship. Cornwall felt this particularly acutely not just because people wanted the status quo in the way they worshipped but also the issue of language at the time. Cornish was still spoken and so the imposition of an English prayer book wasn't just about the process of religion and worship.

It actually kicked off in a village in Devon after a few pints of cider on one festival day. Somebody tried to read from the English prayer book and was beaten to death on the steps. It started a more serious uprising. Exeter was besieged for some period of time, but eventually the King with foreign mercenaries killed many of the rebels and eventually chased them back to the village where it all began.

It was a significant moment for Cornwall. The defeat of that was used to replace a lot of Cornish land owners with English. The provost - the Mayor of St Ives - was taken out to lunch by the King's Commander, but while they were having a meal the troops were building the scaffold to execute him after they'd finished eating. Bodies were left to hang in some of the churches in Exeter and around to remind people: don't do that again. Some were hanging for several years.

The Enclosures

A big change in our countryside was the enclosures. I'm sure there is more to be told about the way enclosures were imposed in our countryside to create the field pattern that we are now used to. 'The law locks up the man or woman who steals the goose from off the common but leaves the greater villain loose who steals the common from off the goose', said one old poem.

There are interesting stories of much more serious rebellions in our forests when there were much more woodlands across the West Country. Forests allowed a different sort of use of the land. Artisans used the wood for carpentry, pit props, barrels, coopering and tanning. All sorts of skilled trades required access to the wood and to the timber.

What is called the Western Uprising happened in the early 1600s. For a period of decades local people smashed down any attempts to enclose the forests around Mere, Gillingham and Warminster. There was a whole community resistance to enclosures. Land around Gillingham and Mere was owned by the First Earl of Elgin who had a hated agent responsible for managing the land called Brunker. Every time he built the fences people smashed them down. When he had someone arrested a crowd would descend on the magistrate and free them.

Civil War

This is a period during the Civil war. The Earl Elgin was a Parliamentarian and when the nearby Wardour Castle battle was taking place Brunker managed to get some Roundhead troops to come and try and put down the local resistance to his enclosures. What he found was that the Parliamentary troops sympathised with the locals. After the tide of the Civil war changed and the Royalist troops were winning, Brunker tried to get them down to try and sort out his local difficulties. That didn't work either. The battles petered out around the 1650s when land for allotments was given for the feeding of the community, but also the trees were felled. In the Forest of Dean the rebellions carried on.

The Civil war swept back and forth. The West Country changed hands several times. The conflict spawned a radical set of ideas across all sort of persuasions. The puritanicals tried to ban Christmas and dancing but there was also a flourishing of libertarian ideas. The Diggers believed that land should be held in common and settlements appeared, many of them put down very quickly. The Levellers, the first socialists, argued for an elected parliament.

Religious non-conformists

In Wiltshire there was a flourishing of non-conformists, dissenting, radical religions. Horningsham Chapel was built in 1566 but many of those that rejected the established church were persecuted.

The Ranters believed in freedom of everything including language and sexual conduct. They often got mixed up with the early Quakers who were also attacked by the State. James Naylor was a Quaker who rode through Bristol on horseback on Psalm Sunday. He then claimed he wasn't re-enacting Christ's entry into Jerusalem but it was seen as a blasphemous act. He escaped execution but instead was branded on the forehead

Horningsham Chapel in Wiltshire near the Somerset border.

with the letter B and his tongue was pierced for this act of blasphemy.

George Fox was the founder of the Society of Friends, what we now call the Quakers. They believed in greater equality, generally in society, including between men and women. They rejected traditions of dress and conduct. They refused to accept the doffing of the cap, the bowing and scraping to one's masters. They refused to pay their tythes and refused to go to church and were often fined. The Quakers became more respectable, but their campaigns for equality and against slavery have put them on the left of religious faith.

The Monmouth Rebellion

The Monmouth rebellion started when the Duke of Monmouth landed at Lyme Regis and his troops headed north, gathering people largely around the freedom to worship against the increasingly intolerant king. They expected to get re-enforcements at Bristol but when those didn't come they realised the game was up. There were a few skirmishes on the way; Norton St Phillip still has Bloody Lane named after where the King's troops were killed, but Monmouth returned back into Somerset, losing deserters along the way. The uprising ended at the Battle of Sedgemoor where it was brutally put down.

The Duke of Monmouth himself managed to escape the battle and was found in a ditch in Dorset. Judge Jeffries led the retribution against those who survived the battle. People were executed in their own villages. Colyton is called the Rebel Town. People were taken back there to be hanged in front of their friends and family. Some were taken to what is now called Monmouth Beach in Lyme Regis to be hanged.

The Duke of Monmouth was executed in London by Jack Ketch. When Monmouth climbed the scaffold he knew that Ketch was a notoriously rubbish executioner and so gave him some money and said, "do a better job than you did of Lord Russell". Jack Ketch took his first swing and made a complete mess of it. A couple more swings later and Monmouth staggered around the scaffold. Jack ketch lost his nerve and soldiers had to insist he finished the job. It eventually took a butchers knife to finish the job. The crowd turned on Jack Ketch and the soldiers had to escort the executioner away.

Smuggling

The West Country is a peninsular and, because it is surrounded by water, smuggling was a large part of the economy. History has so many characters, some of whom were major business folk in their own right and established quite significant operations employing many people. Smuggler's Church in Dorset has a tomb to Robert Trotman, which is engraved with a poem describing him being murdered by the customs officials for smuggling some tea. Tea in one side of the scale and his life on the other. Is this really a fair balance of justice?

The press gang

For about a hundred years Britain was almost continuously at war and the Navy and to a lesser extent the Army was staffed by the press gangs. Men lived not knowing that if they went to the pub they may not come home again. The West Country became notorious for resistance to the press gangs.

The press gang would grab people to be taken to a rendezvous point before

The LIBERTY of the SUBJECT.

being put on tenders, mainly at Avonmouth, to be taken around the coast to Plymouth to join their naval ships. Hundreds of people would sometimes descend on the press gang. Bristol for a while became a no-go area. Some of this was pretty brutal. There was one notorious, press ganger who was a prize fighter and when he chased a target into a pub in Long Ashton the locals set about him, viciously. They broke his ribs, fractured his skull, cut off his fingers and then threw him into the street, fatally wounded.

The press gangs intercepted the merchant ships as they were returning up the channel to capture as many sailors as possible to put them on ships headed back to sea. To avoid this, ships would pull in and let off as many sailors as they could afford to before they came up the channel. Sailors would get off along the Severn shore-line and head inland, particularly around Somerset where they would join up with the miners. There are references in the records such as, "they've gone in with the miners where we dare not follow". This solidarity between miners and sailors was in part because sometimes they were the same people. When you weren't at sea you went down the pit during the winter. The same happened in Cornwall and in the Forest of Dean where the press gangs couldn't really operate because of fierce community resistance. The Hole in the Wall pub is named after the hole where a lookout would watch out for the press gangs coming.

Sailors were let off at Portland before coming into harbour at Weymouth. The press gangs tried to corner them on the island and there is a memorial in Portland Church to those who were killed in a battle with the press gangs. They were quarrymen and blacksmiths trying to protect people. The pilots of Pill were a notoriously rebellious community who piloted the shipping in the estuary. They were often accused of harbouring people escaping the press gangs.

Ships were often death-traps, called 'coffin ships' but sailors who refused to sail on over-loaded ships were imprisoned. Bristol MP, Bristol born Samuel Plimsoll came up with the very simple device of a line so all could see if the ship was over loaded.

Resistance

Rioting was a common form of resistance. There were all sorts: hunger riots, potato riots, cider riots. Without a vote, kicking over the traces was the only way to fight back. This wasn't just drunken mobs throwing stones, it was often well organised resistance to merchants who were profiteering, smashing down grain stores. Miners who needed to get to sell their coal in Bristol resisted the setting of tolls on the Bristol Bridge. Many people were killed. Oyster shells were thrown at the police! Eventually the authorities had to give in and the tolls were abandoned.

Around the 1800s, trade unionism was illegal so strikes often involved a degree of sabotage. Thomas Helliker was an apprentice shearman in Trowbridge, charged and executed for his alleged part in a fire during a strike. He was innocent but if he did know who was involved he refused to testify against his comrades and was hanged on his 19th birthday.

The Swing Rebellion amongst farm

Margaret Bondfield —the first female cabinet minister.

labourers swept southern Britain during 1830 particularly around the poor chalk lands of the Pewsey valley, where wages were the lowest because of the infertile soils. Further into Gloucestershire and Somerset the clay soil allowed a more profitable dairy industry and cheese production. This is where that expression 'the difference between the chalk and the cheese' comes from.

The most serious political rioting in Britain was in Bristol in 1831 after the House of Lords blocked voting reform. There were a number of people killed. We don't really know how many.

Just two or three years later the Tolpuddle farm workers met to discuss how to resist further pay cuts. George Loveless and others concluded that the answer was not smashing machines but forming a legal trade union. The taking of an oath, the bond of solidarity with one another, was the device that Squire Frampton and the Home Secretary used to have them arrested. What we celebrate today is the response to the harsh punishment of seven years' transportation. There was a huge demonstration in London, mass petitions and legal arguments that won the freedom of the six Tolpuddle Martyrs.

There are a lot of untold stories about the fights of women in particular such as the suffragettes. Margaret Bondfield was from Chard. She was a shop worker who rose through the ranks to become the first female cabinet minister. She was a close friend of Florence Hancock.

Julia Varley is another great character who turns up in Chippenham to support milk workers, in Cornwall to help striking china clay workers and then in Chipping Norton in Oxfordshire.

Tony Benn

Tony Benn said that you can't extend your life for more than a minute, but if you study history you can extend it by thousands of years of experience.

Study days like this one, brought together by trades unionists, remind us that we sometimes take for granted aspects of our lives that were won through struggles and rebellions. To quote Tony Benn again: "No issue is ever finally won, no issue is ever finally lost - and we have to keep fighting the same battles every generation".

Further Reading: *West Country Rebels* by Nigel Costley. Published by Breviary Stuff Publications 2012.
ISBN 978-0-9570004-4-4

Chippenham's Trade Union champion

Dame Florence May Hancock
DBE OBE, CBE (1893-1974)

by Melissa Barnett,
Curator, Chippenham Museum

The President of the Trades Union Congress, Miss Florence Hancock, making her inaugural speech, which included an attack on "mischief-mongers"

Everyone likes Miss Hancock, she has no personal enemies. Even those who disagree with her and they are usually on the left, begin by saying, "Miss Hancock is a very nice woman"... what she has done has come from an imperative feeling of duty to her fellow workers.

Observer September 5th 1948

In 1948 Miss Florence Hancock made her inaugural speech as President of the Trades Union Congress. She was only the second woman to achieve this honour in the TUC's then 80 year history.

Although during her life she received honours for her union work and became a Dame Commander of the British Empire in 1951, little has been published about this remarkable woman.

Yet Dame Florence certainly earned her place in British history. Her achievements, causes and the social changes that she championed during her lifetime have affected everyone who lives in Britain today.

A woman of intelligence and compassion, Florence was motivated by the inequality, injustice and the suffering of the ordinary working person and their families. She always saw her union work as being not just to benefit workers in the workplace, but also to improve and enhance their whole quality of life.

Florence was always of the view that the power and influence of trade unions should be involved in politics as a voice to strengthen and improve conditions for the poorest and most vulnerable in society, of which of course she had personal experience. Her main passion was equality between men and women, which she campaigned for all her life.

Florence lived through incredible, changing and often very difficult times. The force of character that drove her hugely successful career in the Trade Union movement was almost certainly forged and influenced by dealing with the problems she saw and experienced all around her during her childhood and early working life.

Early Life in Chippenham

Florence May Hancock was born at 14 Factory Lane, Chippenham on 25th February 1893.

Known throughout her life to her close friends and family as "Flossie", she was the second child of Jacob Hancock and his second wife, Mary Pepler, née Harding, both of whom were weavers at the Waterford Cloth Factory just a couple of doors down from their home in Factory Lane.

The early history of the family is fascinating and shows the measures and mobility that working people had to undergo to survive at this time. Jacob Harding arrived in Chippenham from Wootten-under-Edge, via Upton Lovell, Westbury and Westbury Leigh. Mary Harding was born in South Wales to a Trowbridge family and arrived via Westbury, Bradford-on-Avon and Trowbridge.

Life for the Hancock family in Chippenham was, if not strictly lived in poverty, very difficult and sorrowful. Illness and death were never very far away for the working class at the time.

Chippenham Museum Collection

The girl stands in the doorway of No 8. The post is in front of the doorway to No 7, the one-bedroomed cottage in which a teenage Florence lived with her father, sister and two brothers from 1910 until 1913-1914. The two storey house on the right is the rear of No 14 Factory Lane (Florence's birthplace), which faces the street

Chippenham c1907

The Workers' Union Record commented in 1920 that "Her early life was one long grim struggle with the problem of existence."

When Florence's parents were married in 1890 it was the second marriage for both of them as they had lost their first partners. Her entry in the Dictionary of National Biography states that she was one of 14 children, however there were certainly more and the combined family had at least three infants who died before their first birthday.

For most of her life in Chippenham Florence lived in Factory Lane, although in three different houses.

The area comprising Factory Lane (now Westmead Lane), Blind Lane (renamed Gladstone Road in the 1920s) and River Street was a lower working class area of the town. All the houses that Florence lived in were constructed around 1830 by Anthony Guy for workers at his new Bridge Mill cloth factory

Life for the residents of Factory Lane in the Victorian Period was very different from the lives of those who live there today. At the bottom of Florence's garden was a slaughterhouse. Across the road was a tannery, 50 yards away a cloth mill belched out smoke from its new chimney and behind that was the Gas Works.

Directly across the river the Milk Factory rose with its new chimneys. As both the tannery and the cloth factory used stale urine as a major ingredient in their processes, the stench and pollution from these industries, particularly in the summer, would have been considerable.

It was not just the problems of local industry that the Hancock family needed to cope with. Their homes bordered the River Avon. Chippenham did not have a mains sewerage system until 1898, thus the river itself was the only outlet for waste water, it was an open sewer. In this low lying part of town, when heavy rain caused the frequent flooding for which the town was noted, not only did the River Avon flow past the Hancock family's home, it would inundate it.

Conditions for the family and their neighbours must have been terrible. So much so that when the Borough Council was ordered to begin clearing all the substandard "slum" housing from the town in the 1930s, Factory Lane was where the project started.

Florence entered Westmead School (still known then as the British School) as pupil number 1556 on 4th May 1896. Unfortunately most of the school records were lost in a fire in 1972 so we know nothing of her time there but she would have received a basic, elementary education.

Officially the school leaving age was 14 but, like many families of the period, there was pressure on Florence to begin work as early as possible to bring another, much needed, wage into the household. Particularly as her father was in and out of work, depending on the nature of the cloth trade at the time.

In 1905, aged 12½, Florence achieved the standard required to be able to leave school early and began work as a washer-upper in a local café. Her hours were from 7.00am until 9.00pm for which she earned 3 shillings a week plus food.

Looking back 30 years later Florence remembers her employer as being kindly, but unfortunately she never mentions who it was. She also jokingly referred to herself as a "slavey." However, as she recalls that it was the largest café in town and did the catering for all the large local evening functions, which meant her not finishing until as late as 2.00am, the indications are that it was probably the Waverley Temperance Hotel and Coffee Tavern in the Market Place.

The regulations governing the employment of children at the time, the Employment of Children Act 1903, stipulated that no child under the age of 14 should be employed in any occupation before 6am or after 8pm or for more than nine and a half hours a day, or on a Sunday.This meant that on the evenings when the café was catering for a function they were breaking the law and the police would often raid them looking for Florence! When this happened she was instructed to slip out of the back door to go and hide. Fortunately for her and her employer she was never caught.

By her own accounts Florence was politically motivated at an early age. Her grandfather was a Chartist and her father was a militant radical, pro Lloyd George and anti-Boer war. Her mother was an active member of the Co-operative Society and gained a reputation for heckling at political meetings.

Florence had been reading the *Reynolds's News*, the radical newspaper of the day, to her father on Sunday afternoons since she was five years old and at 10 had gone with him to see Lloyd George speak. There were also readings of the political pamphlets Mr Hancock frequently bought.

In an *Observer* newspaper article written about Florence in 1948, the comment was made that her "socialism is mixed up with the Sermon on the Mount and the Sunday School (we have found that she attended the Tabernacle in Chippenham); the aim is the Millennium and the gentle reign of the brotherhood of man."

Her Socialist mentors were English and romantic, William Morris and Robert Owen. She was offended by the materialism of Marxism. She felt the emphasis in Socialism should not be on how much the State can give to the individual but how much the individual can give to the State. To her, Society was "for giving not of taking"

So as a young girl Florence was encouraged to become politically active. According to her own reports she was also a women's suffrage supporter and helped at local meetings from the age of 14. However then, as later, the emphasis of her politics was on the achievement of her goals through gradual process not militancy.

Working life in Chippenham

In February 1905, as soon as she reached 14, Florence left the café and went to work at the Nestlé and Anglo-Swiss Condensed Milk Factory. Here she worked a 55 hour week, from 7.00am until 6.00pm, five days a week, and then until 2.30pm on a Saturday. Her starting wages were five shillings and ninepence (5s 9d) a week, with a rise each year, sixpence one year, seven pence the next, rising to a top rate of eight shillings and nine pence (8s 9d) when she reached 21. Men in the same factory were paid seventeen shillings and sixpence (17s 6d.)

In 1901 Seerbolhm Rowntree, the

Chippenham Museum Collection

Nestlé and Anglo-Swiss Condensed Milk Factory

social reformer, published his "Poverty, a Study of Town Life." He described what he called the "Poverty Line," the level of income below which it was impossible to live. This he defined as twenty one shillings (21s) for a married man and family.

Florence mentioned that she worked in the first shop the manager passed when he did his factory tour each morning. It seems likely that she was either in the packing department, stacking the filled tins into crates and boxes or more likely the tin filling department pouring the condensed milk from a large jug into each individual tin by hand.

MILK FACTORY WORKERS' STRIKE AT CHIPPENHAM.

DEMAND FOR MORE WAGES AND SHORTER HOURS.

STAVERTON WORKERS DECLINE TO JOIN.

SETTLED !

END OF THE CHIPPENHAM STRIKE.

WORKERS' TERMS ACCEPTED.

Florence was 17 in 1910 when her mother died and it became necessary for her to help bring up her three younger siblings. In 1912 her father became ill, reducing the family income still further, and by her own account Florence had to seek help before the Board of Guardians for poor relief. Not long after, in june 1913, her father died.

Wages and working conditions at the factory were bad and Florence had responsibilities at home. This was not helped by the tyrannical attitude of the factory manager, Fred Rogers, who Florence described as "terrifying". Looking back at this time, she later stated, "If he was bad tempered somebody was for it. I have known him dismiss instantly a worker who had done nothing wrong at all."

By 1913 he was expecting the workers to work 60 hours a week, 5 hours more than they were contracted for, with no overtime pay, at the lowest rates for any factory in the area (two shillings a week lower than at the Beaverton Milk Factory) and the workers, not least Florence, had had enough.

On the evening of Friday 6th January, the workers arranged a meeting in the Temperance Hall in Foghamshire. This was addressed by Julia Varley of the Workers' Union with the aim to establish a branch of the Workers' Union to campaign for better rights at the factory. Only 20 people turned up, 19 men and one woman – the 19 year old Florence Hancock. Deciding to carry on they elected Roland Cook and William Howell as joint secretaries.

Later reports have had Florence as the main instigator, but she never claims this herself. What is certain is that the family were in poor straights at this time and she was determined to do something about it.

Fred Rogers was having none of it. As soon as he got to hear that his workers were trying to better themselves he took action. When Cook and Howell turned up for work the next day they were told their services were no longer required and paid off. Roland Cook had worked at the factory for 16 years.

Throughout the following Sunday the workers campaigned to have the two men reinstated. On Monday most of the workers walked out on strike and went to the railway station to meet Alf Ellery, district organiser for the workers. They marched up to the Bear Hotel where they held a public meeting. Later Ellery was greeted "with thunderous applause," at the Temperance Hotel as he stood up to read out the workers' demands:

- The two dismissed men to be reinstated. (Cheers)
- Factory hours to be reduced from 60 to 55. (Applause)
- The minimum wage for all men over 21 to be £1. (Applause, hear, hear) Wages of youths to rise automatically according to age until they reached 21. (Applause)

On Thursday 16th, ten days later, questions were asked in parliament by the MP Charles Duncan (these are recorded in *Hansard*). Following this bad publicity Fred Rogers conceded to all the demands.

So a group of milk factory workers took on a huge multi-national company and won.

This outcome was historic. Not only was it the first strike by unskilled workers in Chippenham but it directly brought about the birth of the labour movement in the town.

This of course totally changed Florence's life. In the short-term by improving conditions in the factory, with an increase in wages and working conditions. As Florence said: "We were no longer afraid of the boss, which to me was the most important thing of all." It also lead into a life of campaigning on behalf of others, starting with her appointment as the first unpaid dues collector (shop steward) for the Chippenham Branch of the Workers' Union.

The success of the Nestlé workers had a ripple effect across the town and

Chippenham Museum Collection

The first ever joint trade union demonstration in Chippenham, to raise funds for the Cottage Hospital, May 1917.

soon the Union had members in the cloth factory, bacon factory, town mill and the laundry among other places. The road sweepers of the Borough Council joined, and were the first of the new branch to receive a pay rise. Soon there were three branches of the Workers' Union in the town.

Workers joined the Union not just in Chippenham but in all the surrounding towns and villages. This was helped by the outbreak of war in 1914 when the need to turn all of factory output behind the war effort demanded greater organisation. Soon there was a Wiltshire Branch with Charles Humphries, a former baker from Chippenham, as its secretary.

First World War 1914-18

The First World War had many consequences for Florence. She lost two half-brothers, a nephew and her sweetheart in the conflict. It is probably no coincidence that the first "War shrine," remembering both the dead and serving of the town appeared on the corner of Factory Lane in 1917. But the war also brought in rationing, huge price rises, shortages and obvious profiteering.

Despite a mutual agreement with the government not to take industrial action during the conflict (strikes were actually banned under the Defence of the Realm Act 1914) by 1916, when conscription was introduced, there was widespread opposition to the consequences of the war in Wiltshire.

Workers were seeing their friends, work colleagues and family members coming home injured in their hundreds, or receiving news they were not coming home at all. In return for this, they were receiving less relative pay but seeing the factory owners make huge profits. So they began to agitate, led in Wiltshire by Charles Humphries.

When conscription was extended to married men in May 1916, Humphries was one of the first to be called. But if the employers and business owners thought this would stop any union activity or demands for improved conditions from their workers they reckoned without Florence Hancock, who had joined the Independent Labour Party in 1915.

By now Florence had proved to be more than competent to organise the Workers' Union Chippenham branch and so she was offered the position to replace Humphries as full-time officer for the Workers' Union in the county.

This pleased her manager who said she would never be welcome back. Her colleagues however presented her with a gold watch. Officially her title was now "Women's Officer," but she worked organising both men and women. As the union was active not just in the factories but also among farm workers this must have involved bicycling hundreds, if not thousands of miles visiting members.

It was not long before workers at the milk factory gained an extra "War work bonus". In June 1915 a strike began among the girls at Chippenham Laundry and in July at the rubber factory in Melksham.

In September Florence was at a meeting in the Town Hall in Trowbridge, explaining, in a softly-spoken but powerful way, how better organisation could lead to better conditions. At the beginning of the meeting 56 people were in the Trowbridge Branch of the Workers' Union, at the end of it 500 had joined.

The next week she was in Bradford-on-Avon and Westbury and a lifetime career in the trade union movement was underway.

The Workers' Union was one of the more patriotic unions – and hence grew during the war – which gave opportunities for intelligent and motivated people like Florence.

Rank and File Personalities No. 7.

FLORENCE HANCOCK
(GLOUCESTER)
SOCIALIST AND TRADE UNION ORGANISER

THIS IS THE seventh of a series of brief character sketches of rank and file personalities throughout the movement. Contributions to this feature are especially solicited. Almost everyone in the movement knows of at least one such character—a literature seller, a branch secretary, etc., etc. *Don't ask his permission*, but write a brief sketch (500 words) of him, enclosing, if possible, his (or her) photograph, and send it to *The Socialist Review*, 14 Great George Street, Westminster, S.W.1.

FLORENCE M. HANCOCK may not be as widely known as she deserves to be throughout the Socialist movement, but her splendid work, untiring energy, and genial personality have endeared her in the hearts of thousands of workers in the South-Western Counties.

Probably her early life provided the kind of training school best qualified to fit her for the kind of work into which she has thrown her heart and soul. Born of working-class parents, "one of fourteen," she tells us, nine of whom are still alive, losing her mother by death when our heroine was only seventeen, she herself became mother to the rest, and undertook all the household responsibilities. Five years before this sad event she had commenced work as a "slavey" in a restaurant at the age of twelve years. All along the line it was a bitter, cruel fight with poverty and trouble, but she won through without becoming soured or embittered. In her case, great obstacles produced great courage. Readers can imagine for themselves what it meant to "mother" so large a family while yet so young, and how her experiences must have qualified her to enter into a complete understanding of the conditions of working-class struggles. Her father was a real Radical, and frequently it was the duty of "Florrie" to read to him in the evening *Reynolds's Newspaper*, in the days when W. M. Thompson was editor. While in her early 'teens she became enthusiastic-

Socialist Worker

Florence's story moves on from Chippenham to a more national stage after 1918.

She was so successful in Wiltshire that sometime around 1918-1919 she was made Women's Organiser for the Western Region of Workers' Union, working out of Gloucester. She thought long and hard about accepting this job and asked for a month to think it over. She was later reported to have been "afraid of failure, of locked factory doors, of poverty and of strange places", for she did not want to leave Wiltshire.

Information from this period is limited but we know that Florence became gradually more involved in politics.

In 1918 Florence took part in the first Trade Union Summer School at Ruskin College. A year later she attended an organisers conference at Balliol College. There are articles written about her as the rising star at this time.

By 1920 Florence was Secretary and then Chair of the Gloucester ILP (Independent Labour Party) as well as being active in the Labour Party in the

TUC General Council meeting1937. Florence is seated by the double door. She is the only one in the room smiling.

South West. She helped Charles Duncan, general secretary of the Workers' Union to defend his parliamentary seat at Clay Cross but despite these political interests Florence increasingly concentrated her energies on the trade union movement.

There are records of her leading a strike of stick workers in the Stroud Valley (1920) and was a member of the Pin Trade Board. As a speaker on the Union platform Florence was becoming much in demand especially in the West Midlands Division.

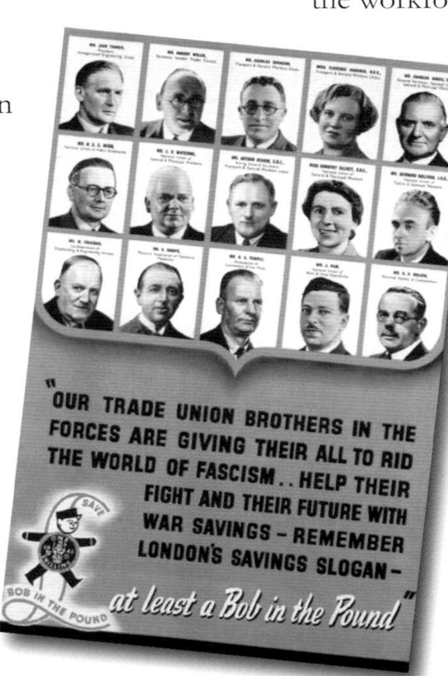

After amalgamation of the Workers' Union with the Transport & General Workers Union in 1929, Florence was appointed Women's Officer for the South West region working from Bristol. A post she held until 1942.

Between the wars she worked hard to organise women in the newly expanding light engineering and consumer industries and was increasingly recognised by her contemporaries.

After much lobbying she was one of the members of the first Trade Union Women's Conference in 1931.

By 1935 she was nominated to the general council of the TUC and in due course served as its nominee to the international labour office, travelling as a delegate to France, Canada and the USA.

Second World War 1939-45

During WW2, Florence was appointed a special advisor to the Minister of Labour, Ernest Bevin. Her remit was to look both at conditions in the wartime factories and to consider how to manage the workforce after the war.

In this role she sat on the organising committee of the Red Cross and St John's Ambulance nursing organisation. She was also the invasion officer for the south west region and was also the union representative on various other government boards.

In 1942 she became Chief Woman Officer of the TGWU, supervising the industrial affairs of some 200,000 women. This was a post she held for 16 years. With Violet Markham she compiled a special report on Women in Domestic Service as this role was seen as key to ensuring that post-war unemployment would be kept under control, unlike in 1919.

She was an advisor to the commission on Equal Pay in 1944 and supported campaigns for general women's rights, such as a national maternity service and free places for nursery schools. She was also a member of a committee on the Juvenile Employment Service.

Post War — President of the Trades Union Congress

Post-war her knowledge and experience of industrial organisation meant she was in frequent demand to sit on and advise public bodies.

In 1947 came her greatest honour, when she was elected to serve as the chairman of the General Council of the TUC, leading onto her holding the Presidency of the TUC General Congress in 1948, only the second woman ever to do so.

Florence's term as President, described as "a chink of light among the gloom", came at a very difficult time for the unions. Post-war Britain was in the throes of runaway inflation, the TUC was forced to choose between supporting the Labour government in its austerity measures and a package for full-employment, or its members' left-wing calls for strikes and militancy. That she supported the call for conciliation and moderation, despite her own inclination to push for greater equality for women, probably led to greater harmony in the long term than might otherwise have been the case.

Her wartime organisational work gained her the nomination of an OBE in 1942 and a CBE in 1947. In 1951 she gained the highest honour that a female commoner could receive, becoming a Dame Commander of the British Empire (DBE).

Retirement

On retirement in 1958 she left London and her villa in south Harrow and moved back to Bristol where she continued her lifelong service to the public by becoming a Justice of the Peace. She carried on campaigning for social equality, and was a Director of Remploy – an organisation that, at the time, directly employed disabled people in a number of factories – until 1966. On 3rd September 1964 she married John Donovan a colleague she had known for 30 years in the TGWU, who had recently been widowed with six grown up children. They honeymooned at the TUC Annual Conference in Blackpool. He passed away in 1971.

Looking back on her career her colleague Dame Anne Godwin noted that Florence "made an enemy of anyone, whether communists, non-unionists or bad employers who sought to undermine the trade union movement". She was a woman of true mettle. Others described her as "brisk, cheerful and good natured... a wonderfully loyal friend and trustworthy colleague, incapable of dirty tricks" (*The Times*, 16 April 1974).

However to her beloved family she was kind "Auntie Florrie" who read Agatha Christie, liked sewing, crochet and cooking, who wore neat suits and still spoke with a broad Wiltshire accent and who, throughout her engaged and eventful life, always looked after and cared for them.

Florence was a regular visitor to Chippenham throughout her life, either visiting her family, as a speaker at local functions and at social events. It was here, at the home of her sister Lily Guest in King Alfred Street, that Florence passed away – just a few hundred yards, but a lifetime away, from where she began it.

From Wiltshire to Westminster

By Jeremy Corbyn
Member of Parliament for Islington North

I want to complement you on putting on a history day with such a fantastic attendance. An event like this gives us all food for thought and a great deal that we can learn from. History is such an important topic and sadly it's often the least understood subject that our children have to study at school. We need to encourage those who make education policy to realise that a real understanding of history is empowering for people and a misunderstanding of history is a disempowerment of people. A real understanding of history can defeat racism. A misunderstanding can encourage racism.

I'm not a local historian and so my memories of living in Chippenham are very personal reminiscences. But I lived here from birth until I was eight years old when we moved to Stafford and then Shropshire. I have very happy memories of that time and I want to draw some lessons from them.

Early family influences

My parents were both scientists. Mum was a science teacher and Dad was an engineer. They were also politically active. They met at the Conway Hall in Red Lion Square in London in the 1930s – opposing fascism. I still have a special affection for speaking at Conway Hall because I imagine them sitting where they did in the third row and I remember my mother telling me that she met Mahatma Gandhi's daughter the late Indira Gandhi at a rally there. It makes those times and those campaigns very real for me.

Dad had been very active in the Labour Party, the unions and Spanish Civil War issues, but he could not join up for the Second World War because he worked for an engineering company in a listed profession.

His employers, Westinghouse, relocated to Chippenham and my parents moved there too, living at first in Greenway Gardens. Before I was born they moved to Kington St Michael and that's where I have my first memories of growing up. A trip into Chippenham was a very major journey on the bus for me in those days. There was a bus every hour – how things have changed. And Chippenham seemed so very big at that time, as places do when you are a small child.

My parents had interesting religious views. Mum was brought up in a very Anglican household but became an atheist very early on. Dad on the other hand became quite active in the Church of England. So they had to compromise about schooling. And they did that by sending me to the Roman Catholic primary school on the Bath Road here in Chippenham! I have clear memories of travelling most of the way on the bus with my older brother and then walking up to the school itself. We used to play games along the way and we would collect all the beer bottle tops left behind by the soldiers who had been drinking at the weekend and then throw them into the bin outside the TA building that was on our way.

I have very vivid memories of growing up in Chippenham and I learnt a great deal from the beauty of the countryside. There was a sense of safety and community in the small village of Kington St Michael.

As a very small child I was allowed to be out on my own on my bike for as long as I wanted. And then, at around 5 o'clock in the afternoon people would come to their front door and say, "Get yourself home Jeremy. Your Mum and Dad will be looking for you." It was as though the whole community was caring for everyone else.

There were some old people in the village who had been victims of the WW1 gas attacks and who were breathing with great difficulty. I found it really interesting to talk to them. They seemed very old men to me at the time and they were, basically, dying of the remnants of the poison gas. But they had interesting stories to tell. I was privileged to hear them.

There was an Italian family who lived across the road from us and they were great friends, particularly with Mum. They had been prisoners of war in Wiltshire during WW2 and decided not to return to Italy after the war, but worked on farms locally and were very popular in the community. There was no animosity whatsoever towards them. They provided us with spaghetti and we gave them orange juice. It was a fair deal we had between us. I remember those as very happy days.

Learning from history

My parents, apart from being very committed socialists and peace campaigners, were also very dedicated to history, particularly archaeology. And we went to various digs of Roman villas and so forth. As a five-year-old I didn't always appreciate being dragged off on a Saturday morning to slither about in the mud in some freezing field with my mother saying, "This is a really important dig." But they certainly made their contribution to history at those digs.

They were also very interested in social history. And later on, after they had moved back to Wiltshire to live in Stanton St Bernard, near Devizes, they wrote a history of the village. It's a very small village on the edge of Milk Hill, overlooked by one of Wiltshire's white horses and its history is probably typical of rural Britain.

Their book really brings to life what was happening in rural communities before the Swing Riots and afterwards too. It captures that sense of solidarity brought on by the industrialisation of agriculture, the enclosure of common land and of the oppression of farm workers. This was the time of mass migration and the depression of farm workers' wages was partly an act of policy to encourage them to go and work in industrialised cities.

The sheer brutality and the appalling

living conditions that existed in that village and indeed many others all across the country is something that our children should understand. They should understand that what we now see as often deeply conservative, idyllic communities all over Britain were in fact centres of most enormous ferment, where people were trying to gain some share of the fruits of the industrial revolution that was happening all around them. Instead they suffered brutal and very short lives.

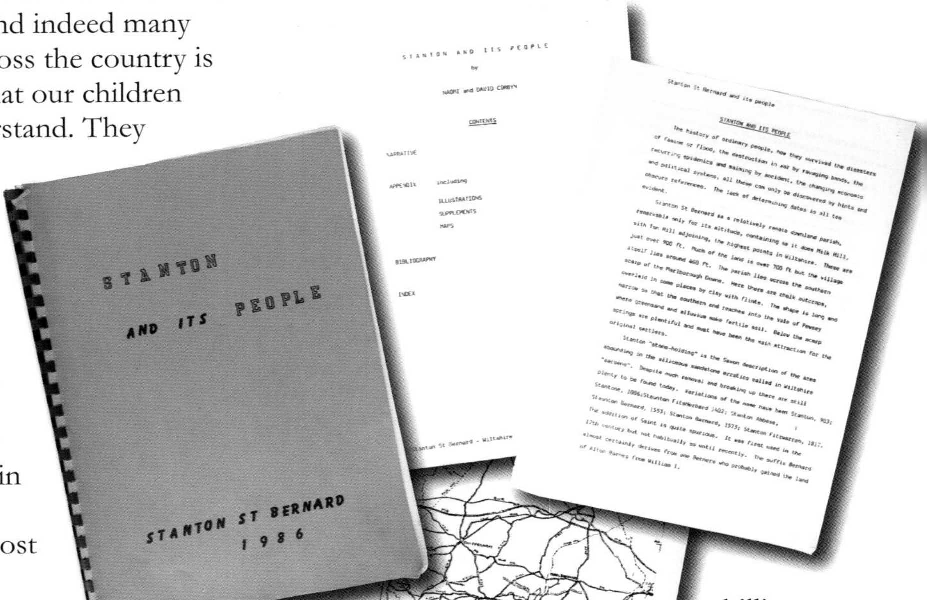

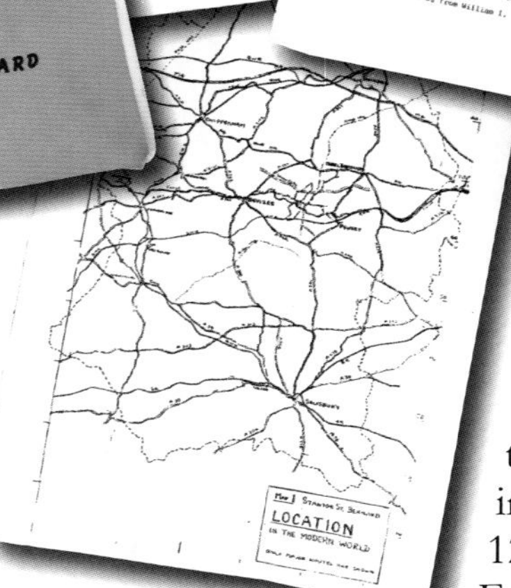

Naomi and David Corbyn's history of Stanton St Bernard

The book quotes the 19th century journalist and politician William Cobbett who wrote about Wiltshire in 1826 in his book Rural Rides. He describes Wiltshire labourers as "the worst used labouring people on the face of the earth. This state of things never can continue many years. By some means or other there must be an end to it and my firm belief is that the end will be dreadful." In his opinion the distress of rural people was caused by: "the dearness of provisions, the scarcity of fuel and the lack of alternative employment."

In 1824 the average weekly wage for an agricultural worker in Britain was 7 shillings and 7d. In Stanton it was only 6 shillings. For comparison, the average wage in Yorkshire was 12 shillings 6d. Further evidence of rural hardship can be seen in the proportion of the community receiving parish relief. In 1830 the percentage in the southern and eastern countries was 10%. In Wiltshire it was 15%.

Cobbett proposed far reaching reforms that included universal suffrage, secret ballots and the setting up trade unions. It is very interesting that he saw the establishment of trade unions as an important part of the solution to rural poverty. His wasn't necessarily a benevolent solution, but a means of empowering the working class of the communities to bring about their own change.

The Combination Law was repealed in 1824 so it might have been possible after that date for the agricultural labourers to organise and defend their living standards as industrial workers were beginning to do. But what happened to the Tolpuddle Martyrs in 1834 shows us how difficult and dangerous it was to take such action.

Nevertheless, agricultural workers did come together to take action when the introduction of threshing machines threatened their winter employment. Riots occurred across the country, machines were broken and hey ricks set on fire. Named eponymously after a mysterious Captain Swing who wrote warning letters to the land owners, the first Swing Riots took place in August 1830 in Kent and spread rapidly throughout southern England, with riots occurring thick and fast in Wiltshire. The Devizes and Wiltshire Gazette reported rick burning at Oare on 19 November and Stanton St Bernard the following day.

Where do children learn about this at school today? They don't. They should!

Political motivation

I hitchhiked to London on a lorry and the driver chose to drop me off on the Holloway Road. So it was chance that took me to Islington, but I stayed in that area and now I'm the MP there. The lorry driver made a good decision that day!

I have always been fascinated by what motivates people to bring around social and political change in our world. There is nothing wrong in looking at what has been achieved in the past as a pointer to what is going to be achieved in the future. This month has been very sad for me personally – and for many of you too I am sure – with the deaths of Bob Crow on 11 March and Tony Benn on 14 March. They were very different people in many ways, but both were incredibly intelligent, very well read, very well informed and both very inspiring. So for all their differences, they were more or less the same people really.

I went to Bob Crow's funeral at the East London Cemetery on Monday 24th. There was a massive crowd, thousands of people lining the street outside the cemetery with banners from unions and all sorts of organisations. So many people saw in Bob someone who stood up for others and they saw their own campaigns and struggles in his death. Bob duly arrived like the East End hero he was, in horse-drawn hearse with Millwall colours on top. The union banners and the Millwall colours reflecting the two very different aspects of his life.

I first met Tony in the late 1960s and I knew him very well indeed. He was a very close friend and we talked frequently. I visited him in hospital shortly before he died. He gave me a big smile and said, "Thanks for coming. Where have you been?" I told him that I had been in the Western Sahara in an act of solidarity with the Moroccan-occupied Sahrawi people. And he said, "Tell me more about that." This is a man who two weeks before his death wanted to learn about other peoples' struggles. He asked lots of questions and then he said, "I haven't long to go. I'm not sure I can last". And I said, "Tony, this isn't acceptable. We spoke before Christmas and you agreed you would go on to 100. You've never let me down before, so please don't this time".

But sadly, Tony has gone. His funeral was also an amazing experience. On one level it was a very traditional service in the church but at another level it was very radical. Religion and the powers of the scriptures were very important to Tony. During the service the Dean said that Tony was always on the side of the prophets against the kings. That really was the story of his life.

In his book Arguments for Socialism, published in 1980, Tony talks about Tom Paine's The Rights of Man, written in 1791 and introducing many of our socialist ideals. He also talks about the Chartists and their origins and quotes from a leaflet issued by the executive committee of the National Chartists Association in 1842 at the time of all the rural uprisings and the start of urban uprising. "The great political truths which have been agitated during the last half century have at length aroused the degraded and insulted white slaves of England" - very strange choice of words – "to a sense of their duty to themselves, their children and their country. Tens of thousands have thrown down their implements of labour. Your taskmasters tremble at your energy and expectant masses eagerly watch the great crisis of our cause. Labour must no longer be the common prey of masters and rulers. Intelligence has beamed upon the minds of the bondsman and he's been convinced that all wealth comfort and produce, everything valuable, useful and elegant has sprung from the palm of his hand. He feels that his cottage is empty, his bank thinly clad, his children breadless, himself hopeless, his mind harassed and his body punished. And undue riches, luxury and gorgeous plenty have been heaped in the palaces of the taskmasters and flooded into the granaries of the oppressor. Nature, God and reason have condemned this inequality and in the thunder of the people's voice it must perish for ever."

Tony managed to translate this into clause 4 of the Labour Party Constitution. He was the most amazing optimist I have ever met. But his understanding of history and the source of power also underpinned his absolute devotion to democracy. He often said, "Grabbing power for power's sake ends up with keeping power for power's sake. And then you don't understand why you are implementing the power that you have found for yourself." And for true democracy there has to be a real structure and accountability.

I enjoyed discussing British constitutional history with Tony and he once said to me, "If you get stuck about the British constitution, go and watch the state opening of parliament and take notice of the order of precedence in which the Queen and others walk into the House of Lords. Therein lies the entire British constitution set out in serried ranks of the unaccountable dictating to us what we must do."

Tony believed that the struggles that took place all around the country from as early as the peasants revolt in the 12th century, right through the Civil War and all the struggles that came later have all eventually been reflected in our national laws and constitution, but each victory, such as the independence of the House of Commons after the English Civil War is always fettered. The House of Commons, for example, does not elect a Speaker. That needs Royal approval.

Likewise, the Sergeant at Arms is a Royal appointment. And this is where the lack of democracy in our society is bedded.

Ironically, when Tony Benn's body lay in state in St Mary's Undercroft, the very beautiful chapel underneath St Stephen's entrance to the House of Commons, the Queen had to give her consent to Tony lying there. I'm not sure he would have wanted that consent.

Welfare and democracy

Tony always believed in the power of democracy and the need for parliament to assert itself as a means of achieving democracy. My view is that we do not live in a totally democratic society. We certainly live in a grossly unequal society, and our society is consistently de–politicised and disempowered because of it.

Peace

Like so many around the country, the War Memorial near the Market Square here in Chippenham lists massive numbers of those who died in WW1, WW2, the Gulf War and the Iraq War – as well, unusually, as the conflict in Ireland. At a glance you can see the tragedy for family after family. Whole lists of brothers and cousins died in those wars.

Tony Benn understood inequalities in power and the need for internationalism and understanding. He was in Rhodesia in WW2 and he saw first hand the disgusting treatment of African workers and farmers. He was a founder of the movement Colonial Freedom, now called Liberation, which I Chair, standing up for the victims in Kenya during the British Colonial war in the 1950s. The Mau Mau people suffered abominable treatment during that time.

It was my privilege to meet some of those victims in 2013. They had been put in concentration camps by the British Army and castrated as a form of punishment. Other vile treatments were also meted out. They finally won not quite an apology but an acknowledgement that they had been harshly treated by the British government. And compensation has been agreed. But compensation can't replace what they have lost.

Tony also opposed the Falklands War in 1982 describing it as essentially a war about minerals and influence in South Africa. Obviously he also opposed the later wars in Afghanistan and Iraq.

We are brutalised by war. But we have been fed a diet that somehow or other our security is dependent on our ability to go to war and that spending £30 billion, losing 1000 soldiers' lives and tens of thousands of other lives in Afghanistan and Iraq has actually made us safer and provided a better society. It certainly doesn't feel any safer for young Muslim people in my constituency since those wars took place - faced as they are with the degree of racism and xenophobia that accompanies all those kinds of things.

What are these wars really about? They reflect the power of very big business to take natural resources from other people. This is no different from the colonial wars all over the world that workers in Wiltshire and elsewhere were sent off to fight all through the 18th and 19th centuries. We must understand the dangers of militarism. I like to acknowledge that parliament voted against going to war in Syria in August 2013. I do not have sympathy for the regime in Syria, but I couldn't see what western forces were going to do there other than sell a great lot of arms to a lot of people. I would like to think that this was a turning point and people are not prepared to get involved in wars on behalf of the USA ever again.

The threat to the welfare state

One of the biggest issues facing us today is undoubtedly austerity and its threat to the fabric of the welfare state.

In the 17th, 18th and particularly the 19th centuries workers in rural areas faced absolute poverty. And there was poverty in urban areas as well. Workers campaigned for higher wages and trades unions played an important part in that. But there was something else pushing for change. Political trades unionism sought to create a welfare system to protect people from destitution, a health system and some security for older people.

In the 1908 People's Budget we got the principles of a national insurance system and with it a very basic health system. After WW2 we achieved the National Health Service and the principles of universal social security. These achievements came from the struggles of those people who dared to stand up against the power of landlords and the unaccountable power of all of the aristocracy on Britain in earlier centuries.

Those achievements are all now at risk. We are being told that welfare spending in UK plc is just another aspect of government spending like anything else. But if we as a society guarantee people against poverty and destitution, then there should be no cap. It's a condition we have agreed upon and I emphatically oppose any proposal to limit welfare spending.

We've seen the horrors of disability benefit assessments leading to people being taken off disability benefits unfairly. In London I see increasing numbers of people sleeping on the streets. That makes me very angry.

We are told that austerity is necessary because of the economic condition that we are in. No. Austerity is necessary for the banks that have been bailed out; for the tax dodgers and for big businesses that can routinely avoid tax. Austerity must not be allowed to destroy the welfare state and National Health Service that was developed by our society to overcome the struggles of the past. We must not allow austerity to take us back to those times where the landlords and aristocracy held all the power.

Democracy

The last point I want to make is about democracy and where our powers come from. If you look back to the struggles that people faced against landlordism, against the unfair distribution of wealth, against the power of the state to murder and execute people and send others off to wars – who fought back against it? It was workers, including workers in rural areas, who fought back against it and formed trade unions.

People were tried for treason in the beginning of the 19th century for supporting the French Revolution. William Godwyn, the father of Philosophical Anarchism, was tried for treason. He was the partner of Mary

Wollstonecraft, a great feminist and brilliant feminist writer, who lived in my constituency.

But eventually things started to change. We got the 1832 Reform Act – limited in many ways, but it was a fundamental change. Then we got the Factories Act. Thirty years later we got a limited form of state education. Then there was the battle for women's suffrage and the right to vote and after that we developed health and safety legislation and factories legislation. Then we got the welfare state in 1948.

These developments and the limited democracy that we have within our society are rooted in protests and the ideas of solidarity within trade unions. And that democracy has brought about better living standards and better rights. The strengths that we enjoy in our society today came from peoples' struggles over the years. They were never handed down from above.

Nobody ever sat around in the tea room in the House of Commons and said it would be a good idea to have a National Health Service, when shall we do it? They sat around – they still do – and say, "They're all complaining. They don't like us. So we've got to do something about it to get elected again." It is all a question of political pressure.

Conclusion

When we have a day like this to study the history of rural struggles, we can begin to understand how much people sacrificed to achieve what they did by fighting back against inequality, making increasingly brave stances and being executed for it. Public executions were a form of intimidation of the whole community and it took immense bravery to try to free someone on the way to the gallows. But those who carried out the executions became fearful of the way the mob might protest. And things changed. So all those brave people achieved a great deal.

It would be a terrible thing to bring up another generation to believe that all that matters is consumerism and pageant and personality - not to worry about the environment in which they live, the powers they have in society or the opportunities that they have.

We all have to stand together and I'm really pleased to see that you have copies here of the pamphlet Truths and Lies about Migrants produced by South West TUC, because this is the new lie that is being put about – that all our problems are being brought about by immigration. This is nonsense. Our problems are caused by inequality within out society, the waste of our society on wars and the unaccountable power of those who destroy the environment not only here but all over the world through mining and other operations.

We can learn a great deal from history. And by learning from history we can achieve a better and much more decent society and bring up our children to understand that they have to protect what we have achieved, but also demand a great deal more because that in the end is what will bring about the peace and justice that we all crave.

And for me, growing up in a little village in Wiltshire taught me a great deal about environment and people and community. And it's something that will never leave me for the rest of my life.

The Speakers

Rosie MacGregor is Secretary. of the White Horse (Wiltshire) Trades Union Council, and an active member of UNISON, having been South West Regional Convenor of UNISON for 10 years until 2009, during which time she spoke on a variety of public service issues on numerous platforms including the Trades Union Congress.

Steve Poole is Professor of History and Heritage at the University of the West of England and Director of its Regional History Centre. He has published widely on popular culture and social protest in 18th and 19th century Britain, much of it with a regional focus on South West England.

Nigel Costley is the Regional Secretary of South West TUC. He is a well informed campaigner and as the voice of the TUC is one of the most respected and influential speakers in the region on subjects ranging from the regional economy, migrant workers, housing, Europe, the environment, industrial relations and the history of the trade union movement.

Jeremy Corbyn MP has been the Member of Parliament for Islington North since 1983 and Leader of the Labour Party since 2015. His early years were spent in Wiltshire.

Melissa Barnet, Curator of Chippenham Museum is inspired by Dame Florence Hancock who was born and raised Chippenham. She feels honoured to publicise such a remarkable and courageous life. There are plans for a blue plaque in honour of Dame Florence to be erected in Chippenham .

Picture by Bob Naylor: Watermarx

From Left, Rosie MacGregor, Jeremy Corbyn MP, Prof Steve Poole, Nigel Costly and Melissa Barnett